TRUCE COUNTRY

Truce Country

Sue Hyon Bae

EYEWEAR PUBLISHING

POETRY

First published in 2019
by Eyewear Publishing Ltd
Suite 333, 19-21 Crawford Street
Marylebone, London W1H 1PJ
United Kingdom

Cover design and typeset by Edwin Smet
Author photograph by Sue Hyon Bae

Printed in England by TJ International Ltd, Padstow, Cornwall

ISBN 978-1-912477-84-5

*The editor has generally followed American spelling and punctuation
at the author's request.*

WWW.EYEWEARPUBLISHING.COM

For my English teachers—
Miss Mahina, Miss Angelina, Miss Fanny,
Miss Miriam, Miss Hazel, and Mr Grant;
and my parents.

Sue Hyon Bae
was raised in South Korea, Malaysia,
and Texas. Her co-translation of
Kim Hyesoon's *A Drink of Red Mirror*
was published in 2019.
She lives in Phoenix.

TABLE OF CONTENTS

I

AUTOBIOGRAPHICAL — 11

ITINERARY — 12

HELP, I'M IN LOVE WITH RACIST OPERA — 13

THE AUTHOR — 15

AFTER THE THREESOME, THEY BOTH TAKE YOU HOME — 16

GOOD ENGLISH — 17

THE TIME OF SURPLUS — 21

ALONE BUT NOT LONELY — 22

II

MISREMEMBRANCE — 24

III

CITIES & HOMUNCULI — 36

PENNY TRAGEDIES — 38

I AM WAR STUPID — 40

MORNING TOGETHER — 42

PAIN — 43

RESURGAM — 44

ALONE BUT NOT LONELY — 45

IV

TOOTH-SIZED JOYS — 48

V

ALONE BUT NOT LONELY — 60

JEANS AS A METAPHOR — 61

SLOWLY THE MILITARY INVADES EVERYONE — 64

GEN $\sqrt{2}$ — 67

THE BEAUTIFUL COUNTRY — 68

THE DRILL — 71

HIGH SCHOOL BIOLOGY — 72

THERE BUT FOR THE GRACE — 74

THE FLAMMABLE CITY — 77

THE PRACTICAL TABLE OF ELEMENTS — 78

AMERICANA — 79

OURLAND — 80

WE THE PRESIDENT — 81

ANNIVERSARY — 82

RICOCHET — 84

NOTES — 86

ACKNOWLEDGEMENTS — 87

I

I

AUTOBIOGRAPHICAL

When you ask me how I met
the man I loved I'll tell you
the truth, more or less,
substituting *coffee shop* for *internet,*
romantic weekend for *he gambled*
there so much
they comped him a room.
The worst moments aren't choreographed
in appropriately dim rooms
in hospitals and funeral homes. Mine
have been on public transportation,
McDonald's, that time I crossed the Mississippi
by accident. Life and its luminous details
refuse to dissolve. The world goes cheerfully on,
tactless to tragedy, the weather
fails to fit the mood. I want
to tell you the truth about the last time
I saw my mother cry, but we ended up
at a pizza place. Her swollen face was framed
by TV screens showing a baseball game. We
ate dessert. I prefer to tweak and falsify,
meet the demands for how-it-ends.

ITINERARY

For weeks before the trip, you anxious-dream
an infinite airport, dragging along
a suitcase unspeakable, always
in the wrong terminal, following
blurred signs that say Turn Right.
Everything has gone wrong, so you agree,
Turn Right. On the fifth leg
of a centipedal trip, only your left foot
is in this city, your right foot gone ahead
to the next layover. Turn Right.
You are moving out in a spiral. Turn
Right. You are conducting
a spiral search pattern of the world.
Logically, it can't fail. All of you
will be, eventually, where you need to be.

HELP, I'M IN LOVE WITH RACIST OPERA

There are many critically beloved racist operas
but I especially love *Turandot*.
It's embarrassing: It's not Puccini's best,
was left incomplete at his death, promotes Orientalism,

perpetuated yellowface, sentimental storyline,
random dead slave girl. I first saw it
in the DVD recording with the psychedelic David Hockney set
meant to represent Beijing (*Popolo di Pekino*

we become), clownish cheongsam, but
I love it.
I imagine an International Turandot Board
with whom I might sign a contract:

Enjoyment of *Turandot* does not mean its views
reflect my own. ITB, I'm tired of feeling guilty
when the only one wronged in this transaction
is me. ITB, hasn't it been long enough? If I can read

Japanese novels without feeling like a bad Korean,
can't I watch pre-Said Orientalism
without feeling like a bad Asian? Can I endorse
only the parts I like? Will you fund my ideal staging?

Act I, skip to Nessun Dorma, curtains,
forty minutes total. Act II begins
with a trio of slapstick officials named Ping, Pang, Pong;
Act III makes no sense.

Act I gathers suspense like a scream building in my throat.
It forces me to breathe deep in tandem with Calaf
as he rears in shock at our first mutual glimpse
of Princess Turandot the pure, even though

she's usually an oversized white woman
in hideous makeup. It doesn't matter;
she's Turandot, accompanying motif and all.
Act I focuses on Calaf, the idiot prince who ignores

his blind aging father, the pining slave girl, and in some productions,
the heads of Turandot's other suitors on spikes, to shout
 Turandot, Turandot, Turandot
and swing his life into the gong.
We the people of Peking burst into song.

THE AUTHOR

The lawyer retired to a cottage
to write his memoir. His lamp ran on moonlight.
His chair creaked with spite.

He knew all the chapter titles:
The Carpenter Who Climbed An Ice Ladder
A Shopping Bag of Heart Attacks
Frowning Song for Addicts
Navels and Umbrellas and Hot Plates
The Spy Who Sold His Copyright

I think he lived alone
in his cottage. I believe he once had a wife,
a lepidopterist unfurling antennae with forceps.
In his book, he pretends she is the secretary.

AFTER THE THREESOME, THEY BOTH TAKE YOU HOME

even though it's so very late
and they have to report to jobs
in a few hours, they both get in the car,
one driving, one shotgun, you in the back
like a child needing a drive to settle into sleep,
even though one could drive and the other
sleep, because they can't
without each other, they'd rather drive you
across the city than be apart for even a half hour,
the office buildings lit pointlessly beautiful
for nobody except you to admire the reflections
in the water, the lovers too busy talking
about that colleague they don't like,
tomorrow's dinner plans, how once
they bought peaches on a road trip and ate and ate
until they could taste it in each other's pores,
they get out of the car together to kiss you goodnight,
you who have perfected the ghost goodbye,
exiting gatherings noiselessly, leaving only
a dahlia-scented perfume, your ribcage
compressing to slide untouched through doors ajar,
yesterday you were a flash of white in a pigeon's blinking eye,
in the day a few hours old you stand solid and full
of other people's love for each other
spilling over, warm leftovers.

GOOD ENGLISH

1

When I am complimented
on my English,
     I do not feel complimented.

When a classmate marvels that my vocabulary
includes special words like *putrefaction*,
it is not a compliment.

When the receptionist at the dentist tells me
  You don't have an accent
because she doesn't know we both have
accents, it is not a compliment.

When someone who uses greengrocer's
apostrophes doesn't know
about the existence of the subjunctive
in English and believes he has the right
to judge what I say and write
because he was born to our language

  says *Your English is so good*
the foreign tongue in my mouth twists:
No. My English is fucking brilliant.

2

The first English sentence
I learned was   *Who are you?*

from a textbook
written by Koreans translating
literally, who didn't know
that's not how polite English
speakers identify each other.
The first dictionary I memorized
had a pink cover and an example sentence
and illustration for each definition, e.g.

>*She walks among the flowers*
>for *among* accompanied
>by a drawing of a woman in a pink dress
>floating through tulips.

The first English picture book I read
was about a witch named Meg. The first
English non-picture book I read was
about a mermaid named Belinda. I do not remember
my first dream in English,
my first time blurting *Ouch* instead of *Aya,*
the moment my plastic brain flipped the switch.

3

My pronunciation of my mother tongue
is strange. This could be
because English divides sounds
into fewer syllables
and/or because English tongues
live closer to the teeth. In truth,
I am no longer capable of hearing my own strangeness.

4

When I moved to the United States,
I failed the oral English
placement test administered
by my Texas school district
because I could not add up
how much money
the numberless drawings
of American coins
represented
or in what season a holiday
associated with a fat vulture-like bird
is celebrated. I spent one day in ESOL
before a written exam moved me
into a mainstream class
where I was taught to avoid
should of and *could of*,
phrases I had never known before.

5

In eighth grade, I was obsessed with the American
Civil War and could draw from memory
troop movements on each day
of the Battle of Gettysburg. Sometimes I wish
I had stuck with it so that I could have been
the Asian lady historian who shows up at reenactments
correcting men about their armament. Instead,
I teach white teenagers Aristotle's means of persuasion,
which I suppose is cognitively dissonant
still for some of them.

6

Your English is so good feels like being complimented
on how well I breathe
         feels like being catcalled
                  feels like being handed
a plastic cup when everyone else
has champagne flutes. Every time I toast
with champagne, I want to clink my flute
against someone else's so hard they both
shatter into spangles on our feet. Every time
someone begins *Your English*
                          my tongue melts
in my mouth like rancid butter.

THE TIME OF SURPLUS

America said   There's a cheese surplus
If you're a god-fearing patriot   eat more cheese
July said   There's surplus summer
Go forth and exercise your freedoms
You said Want to see a picture of me
in drag? I said Yes and Omg
ur pretty cute   You were amateur
and sweet   America said
Gas is cheap   Get a car
Get two cars   The diner said
An entire potato's worth of home fries
with every meal   The politicians said
We're winning this thing   The philosopher said
Every aesthetic choice is an ethical one
America said   There's all this
ownerless property   Come take yours
We woke every morning saying   Yes

ALONE BUT NOT LONELY

The Business Trip

I wish I could take you with me to these things   felt like

a lonely spork at a fancy restaurant   ate my fancy antelope

off a round slab of tree   guessing by the rings   older than you

couldn't even drink a lot   the cops here insane   inside of the meat

color of hickeys   you shudder into existence around the empty pillow

in fever   forehead smoldering on my shoulder   murmuring

buy me ice cream   the most expensive flavor   let's go out

for a double feature   let me break

     just one of your fingers

II

MISREMEMBRANCE

But where did the train come from?

Reminders of dismemberments:

Gloves as gags. Blank faces of blurred
newsreaders. Distempered dog
foaming. Pretenders to the throne.
Machinery whose parts twist together.

     The mind maims
     when the facts aren't enough –

I swear this is all true: I remember perfectly,
myself at my grandmother's,
chewing dinner as slowly as possible,
watching the evening news:
the boy in the hospital bed
saying he forgave his father,
reporters live from the scene
providing voiceover to the rundown
neighborhood, poor people's insurance
scams, and then, because they had no footage
of it, an artist's sketch
of the boy's leg
on the railroad tracks.

And besides the facts of the case,
I remember my own indifference.
It wasn't that I was too young: I understood
that this handcuffed man crying on TV
had maimed his child for money. No one
had ever hurt me, no one I knew
openly hurt other people, but I wasn't surprised
or disbelieving. I didn't really feel sorry for the boy.
I thought he was dumb for lying himself down
on the tracks just because he was told to,
for lying about it, for forgiving anybody
for the loss of the leg, even if it was his dad,
maybe because it was his dad.

Still, the story made an impression.
There are few news stories I remember
from my childhood in Seoul: the bridge collapse,
the department store collapse (someone I knew
was almost in it), a compilation of politicians
punching each other in green-carpeted Parliament,
the boy with the leg.

I never talked about it.

For years, I didn't think about it.
One of those things you forget
you ever knew, until something
reaches in with a pin and pokes
a dusty part of your brain:

the film *Pietà*. My mother complains
this director leaves her feeling grimy
but she watches with me, transfixed:

the loan shark's enforcer
uses the debtors' own machinery
against them. Each limb insured.

When I say, finally, *Remember that story*
about the little boy who was my age,
whose father—? She replies,
No, it was a finger. Only a finger.
She says, pityingly,
You must have been traumatized.

I research. I have to look up
words in the English-Korean dictionary:
I know *finger* and *insurance*
but have forgotten *amputation*.

I start
with the finger version. I've heard

stories about false memories, I understand
childhood memories are really
retrospective collages.

Still, it's a relief when nothing shows up.
Factory workers getting fingers
crushed or sliced off, boys
called up for military service
cutting theirs off.
Ordinary accidents and crimes.

I should have left it there.

But I'm good at this. I add
a fourth search term,
buja, which usually means *rich*,
but here is a different homonym,
father-son

and fuck, it was a finger.

I didn't remember the scissors at all.

It should be good news—a child
hurt less than I remembered.
But now I have to question

my memories. From where
and why a train?

The loan shark's enforcer had a motive
for dismembering: it's his job.

In *Pietà*, a young man agrees to the severance
of an arm. Asks for it. He needs the money.
He will become a father next month. One arm
will only be enough to pay the debt. He asks for both arms.

The enforcer says *Bureupda—I envy—*
In the Korean sentence the object can be left unsaid:
I envy your child whose father will make
such sacrifices / I envy you for having the capacity
to love this much.

A Korean TV show that tracks down old freak stories
finds the father and son again after ten years.
The father served only four months in prison
and now lives on his son's disability payments,
having forced him to pretend to be mentally ill.

Another man, about to be pushed
off a building, says *I'd rather be dead
than a cripple. Who will look after
my mother?* The enforcer
won't let him go up to the highest level.
Death complicates the claim.

Means of support:
Legs. Flat shoes. Wheelchairs.
Footrests on wheelchairs.
Warm knitted sweaters that cover
the wrist. Bras. Arms.
Chairs. Cages to raise
chickens, rabbits. A truck.
Democratic government.
A pillar in a building. Pillars
under bridges. Parents. Adult children.
All of these things are removable.

The enforcer's name is Lee Kang Do,
which is a homonym for *this thief.*
He takes, among other things,
a bra, ripped right off a woman,
which he uses to whip her
before shoving her husband's arm
into their livelihood, a greasy machine.

Everyone has beautiful hands
and wears dark clothes.
When they hug, their fingers
stand out stark, skeletal,
over the expanses of each others' backs.

A woman says to the enforcer
Plant me a tree. I imagine something
with long breakable limbs, symbolic gestures.
It's only a baby pine, shorter
than the bodies buried under it.

I tell myself: *Even if it were just a finger*
I still wouldn't forgive, even if,
especially if, it had been my parents.
But of course my parents
wouldn't. How can I know
what I would be capable of?

The enforcer holds a lump of brown-red meat
on the tip of his knife and says
If you're really my mother, eat this.
Blood running down his left leg.
She does. Her fingers flutter
to her lips but she doesn't stop chewing.

At least, I think it was the left leg.
If anyone says otherwise, I won't argue.

All of these stories, real and imagined, are about
sons and parents. I suppose the love
of daughters is less in doubt—
therefore, less interesting. It's true
that I am a simple daughter with a simple story:
two parents, four grandparents,
eight aunts and uncles, all more or less
good people. They are kind to me
in their ordinary ways. I believe
they would still be the same
in extreme circumstances. I believe
with faith, without proof.

I thought, at first, the misremembering
was what bothered me. But I don't know—
I believe in my fallibility. The importance
of being a skeptic. My mind fails me,
frequently, often predictably.

And it doesn't bother me that I made the story
more morbid than it was. Everyone knows
children are creepy creatures.

I still think the kid with the finger is dumb, but who knows
how well I would have held up to such a parent. I regret
whatever it is in me that says
the leg story was better—
more dramatic, neater.

The enforcer wants to do something nice for his mother
on his birthday. He asks, *Is there anything you need?*
Anything you want to do? Anyone you want killed?

No one would aspire to this kind of love.
But I can imagine on a smaller scale:
if ever I have to feed my parents
I think I would take extra care buying the meat,
choose the best flesh that will become their flesh.

III

CITIES & HOMUNCULI

I dreamt a city with a copy
of itself in its center in perfect
miniature. On Sundays its citizens
circumambulated around themselves,
the replica throbbing with its own
strollers circling the streets of their city.

It was a *turtles all the way down* city,
an infinite series of identical copies
differing only in size. My own
perception sat on top of the perfect
top layer, where they observed themselves
condescendingly, being topside citizens.

Then I woke and saw that the citizens
around me were also like the city,
that they were infinitely folded themselves
but not identical, because their copies
were inexact, increasingly imperfect.
It looked as if they had put in flaws with their own

hands. Then I examined my own
body and found that I, too, was a citizen
of the infinite city. With perfect
economy I was filled like the city.
The membrane thinness of each copy
allowed uncountable people fitting themselves

into me, and of course each were themselves
brimming with differences of their own.
I heard my old voices from older copies,
the non-rhotic and rhotic citizens
spoke together. From a minute city
someone read the Pearl Poet in perfect

Mancunian. Several miles down, the perfect
structure began to waver as the layers themselves
saw they did not have to stay in their cities.
They could fold up and investigate their own
miniatures, refuse to stay on their levels, be citizens
of other replicas. They began to engender copies,

to perfect thoughts and lives of their own.
Then they themselves dreamt they were citizens
of an infinitely folded city, in which walked their copies.

PENNY TRAGEDIES

Arthur Miller wanted to write a tragedy starring an Everyman,
and so he did, and so Willy Loman is tragic,

and so is Miller's wife Marilyn who
didn't like how they all thought she was marrying

above her intellectual weight, and so is Joe DiMaggio,
who stepped up to organize his ex-wife's funeral,

and so is the way he used to abuse her, tempting
to separate him into old Joe and better Joe

but we must not, so is every frame of unused footage,
so are dogs in love with children who are frightened of them,

so is the Saturday morning in October when I stood alone
with brown Mississippi water crawling at my back,

so is Tennessee Williams' grave, because it is permanent proof
they wouldn't let him follow Hart Crane into the sea, and also

my cousin's dead grandfather's favorite shade of lipstick,
every finger that flips hair onto a bald spot,

and every time a brand-new astronomer discovers that the dome
of the Harvard observatory opens up into a rectangle instead of

two petals unfolding to a round pool of stars with the moon smack in the center
—attention must be paid! That square sky broke my heart.

In fact, here is the only non-tragic detail so far:
when Hart Crane's drunk and bruised body hit

the Gulf of Mexico, there was an orchestral shout,
like the full cannon version of the 1812 Overture

condensed into a splash.

I AM WAR STUPID

Being raised in truce country makes everything simple
    That land across the border
    will be our country someday soon
    Their beliefs are wrong
    Their children are pitiable
    Aren't you lucky to go to school
    where you don't have to catch rats for homework
    You are privileged
    to have textbooks

There is a Wiki page titled *United States military deployments*
It says there are US troops in more that 150 countries
There's a table with the exact numbers
except they don't bother listing countries
with *fewer than 100 personnel deployed*
Did you know the US sent 300 troops to Cameroon last year?
Maybe you did
Maybe it's just me who is war stupid
(who am war stupid?)
It almost makes me miss 7th grade Texas History
All the war causes and war effects fit in worksheets in purple folders
and the only number to memorize was 1836

There's another Wiki page titled *List of ongoing armed conflicts*
with a table of deaths by country
labeled with green and red triangles
noting increase and decrease
like the stock market

Maybe I would be a better human
if I read Al Jazeera
If I phoned my senator
(but do I want what McCain wants?)
If I took some poli sci courses
If the universe said *Here is suffering*
You help carry the load
and I could hold out my hands
to receive a physical weight

MORNING TOGETHER

Today, with no work to do and nowhere to go, I feel
in the process of morning, a slow deliberate action that takes hours.

I morn daringly, dragging the recycling bin to the curb
dressed not quite decently. I morn loose-haired and barefoot.

A neighborhood cat is asleep on the hood of my girlfriend's car.
That's how I know she's my girlfriend; the animals who know me

know her, too. I morn as productively as I can
in this sunlight, washing mugs to make coffee—

I don't clean up before she comes over,
another sign. She morns with me even though she doesn't love

the early calm like I do, for the sake of spending more waking hours
with me. Next year, we'll learn to morn with others,

or alone. But today, she's cross-legged on the worn sofa,
my nail polish collection arranged on the coffee table,

pasting pale green on her nails. It doesn't suit her square fingers,
but still, it's inviting, the way she casually takes over my house

and belongings, how that signifies possession, the thought
of later, hands warm from holding hot mugs,

showing her how to apply the top coat.

PAIN

I type *pain* into the search box, wanting images
of others hurting like I am, or even more, as if schadenfreude
would alleviate the body's demand to dissolve itself.

Instead, the laptop shows me lots of bread.
French boulangeries, loaves dusted white on top, round mounds
with knife cuts showing yellow inside, asymmetrical rolls.

I would like to hug one of the baguettes
and eat it standing in front of the radiant oven.

When I was seven, I thought writers
wore peacoats and fingerless gloves at their desks
because they couldn't afford to heat

their garrets above bakeries. My room is cold, too,
because I can't get out of bed to turn off the AC.
If only I had a loaf of bread

that I could tear in half, scoop out the airy insides
to eat like cotton candy, I would be healed.

RESURGAM

Today I am not reborn from death as I am every morning—
the corpse body no longer mine.

I think, *Rise*; nausea rises instead. The cat calls for me in the yard,
lands like a peeping tom on the windowsill

of the house that looks dead, blinds down,
house blind, unlit in the morning dark,

the day's broth and porridge unmade,
trash fermenting in the kitchen

as the garbage truck clangs near. Let them come,
let them put the house on auction as the deceased's estate,

let them move in, let them repaint, clear out
the cobwebs in the barbecue grill, the gray dough

from the abandoned baking, the body embedded
in the mattress. Let the house be born again.

ALONE BUT NOT LONELY

The Shopping Trip

A devil gives me a piggyback ride

To the supermarket. My skirt rides up

But no one catcalls, not even

At that intersection where someone always honks.

He pushes the cart for me. Celery,

Apples, and it takes me three loops to find walnuts.

He doesn't complain. He is

The kindest man I have met, his gentleness

As unnerving as unexpected affection

From a terminally ill acquaintance.

I should like to be a birthmark on his cheek

Instead of being as helpless as a moon.

Dear Sir, when you hold open

The door, please don't look

So inviting. Don't let me go.

IV

TOOTH-SIZED JOYS

Six years ago, you spent more time sucking silverware than
eating: your tongue fitted into the bowl of the spoon—the metal
tasted better than anything on the spoon.

It takes most of March to realize you are happy. You didn't
recognize the condition at first—you forgot its possibility.

Small joys are preferable to ecstasies: you can fit
more of them in your mouth, carry them with you longer.

Such as:

Picking up a coffee mug to take it to the sink and finding
an inch still warm.

The medical term is *pica: a pattern of eating non-food materials, such as dirt or paper.*

You didn't actually eat any metal: you were still mostly your logical self. Ingestion wasn't the point.

The point was *taste*. An almost spicy bitterness on the tongue.

You keep a record of your small joys.
When putting them in words, you chew them over
like cud. Later, you can look at your own testimony
and know that this was once possible. May be
possible again.

The neighbors divorce:

> *shame — shame on you — bad mother*

You feel neither embarrassment nor sympathy. This being happy business
feels selfish—the sadness of others doesn't touch you—but how long you spent
carrying sadness that belonged to no one.

Take a load off—

You refrained from licking anything that would be socially or hygienically unacceptable. But you imagined how good they would taste:

Door handles. Rusted window frames. The hinges of your roommate's cello case. Faucets on public bathroom sinks.

That last one is what made you mention it to your psychiatrist.

You refuse to feel guilty—happiness
isn't a zero-sum game: when you gain it,
you haven't stolen it from anyone else.

I assume you aren't pregnant, she said.

You take an interest in your surroundings
like a dog giving everybody a thorough sniff.
Things you didn't know you had stopped seeing
reanimate:

The boys behind you talking
like a bad movie dialogue: one says
you know, the yooze—
when you realize he's shortened
usual there's a sudden
exhilaration: it's definitely
the best conversation you've
ever eavesdropped on.

                                       A different doctor said, stern and impatient, you
must eat lunch. At least a protein bar.

                                       Which turned out to be good advice: protein
bars were delicious: metallic powder.

Later, when you were better, you bought a protein bar for old time's sake and were so
disappointed when it didn't taste edible or even seem desirable.

You also drank a lot of iron-enriched orange juice, the type that tastes nothing like real oranges. For a week you drank only this, no water. You drank it from a coffee mug you rarely washed and held each sip in your mouth until it was warm liquid metal.

You recognized that these were unnatural joys that must be rejected.

Note to self:

The protein bars / juice you hold in your mouth are themselves providing nutrients to restore your health, to dim metallic joy.

Try not to miss it.

And:

Your friend's chihuahua,
previously fish-breathed,
has had six rotten teeth extracted
from the left side of his mouth:
the gap makes his lip lift
in a permanent sneer—
preposterously adorable in such a face.

There was another solution to the pica: stop taking antidepressants. Nobody suggested this solution.

Pica:
caused by poor nutrition:
caused by not eating:
caused by poor appetite:
caused by antidepressants (sertraline (Zoloft))
caused by your decision that death-longing was no way to live.

Your brunch partner tells you
the gender neutral for waiter/waitress is
waitron. Together you pretend
the diner is staffed by androids. You
ask your waitron for extra gravy.
It arrives in a teacup.

The first time you filled your prescription, the pharmacist chanted to you the side effects, many contradictory: weight gain, weight loss, increase in suicidal thoughts, mania.

Anorexia. Not anorexia nervosa. You knew every time you looked at your wrists that you were undesirably thin. Nothing tasted.

And your ability to notice colors
de-atrophies:

bougainvillea petals huddled
like trash, purple tissues
trampled by smokers
gathered outside the library.

You stopped eating lunch and started rating metallic objects on how delicious they looked. You shared this with your doctor, as calmly as possible.

You also told your doctor about the night sweats, waking before dawn, vivid dreams.

And browsing books in that library:

Opening *Phaedo*, as you have meant to do for years:

When the poison reaches the heart, that
will be the end:

From out the foxed page a liver-spotted hand plunges into your face and
as it presses down your throat the walls of your esophagus grow mother of pearl—
your bronchi sweat silver—
it runs down your bronchioles—
it illuminates your lungs into many-branched trees—

You also experienced vertigo on stairs. By then
you liked the medication too much, so you didn't
say anything. You didn't know the unsteadiness
had become part of you.

Last winter, you had no health insurance,
so you turned to Marcus Aurelius.

You wrote meditations addressed to yourself.
Mostly about how your boss probably
didn't hate you specifically.

Understand that the world is not malicious
towards you. It simply doesn't care
for individuals.

Today you weigh exactly 105 pounds.

You walk up and down stairs and experience
permanence. You are older than you ever imagined
you would be.

In college, you were always in the 90s, trying so hard for 100. A nice, complete number. At the end of semesters, you force-fed yourself ice cream, trying to fatten up before going home.

The two saguaros in the front yard,
growing together
with their arms, used to look
as if they were fighting. Now they seem to be
caressing each other's faces.

V

ALONE BUT NOT LONELY

The OB/GYN Trip

You heard the clatter of something metal drop on the ground,
you heard him pick it up, but you never heard him put it down.

Maybe he had a light touch, or the tool went on a towel.
Still you imagine it

lodged in you. You make dinner
standing in a skirt with no underwear, waiting.

You press your face into your knees,
wondering whether and how you should investigate.

By now it's the same temperature as you, so it doesn't burn with cold.
It's clamped together, so it doesn't pinch you.

But you feel the stuttering click, muffled,
and its wide weight.

It's hard to find a comfortable position to sleep.
Lying on your side, you see how the arms of the speculum

match the movements of your legs. You absorb
the metal. You grow a green patina.

JEANS AS A METAPHOR

The label of his favorite jeans
                         says Relaxed & Straight
    He says What more do you want in a guy
The label of my favorite jeans says
                         skinny superlow

    He puts his hand
        up one leg hole and laughs
        at how snugly it fits his forearm

The jeans he wears to the office
    tear at the right knee   I say
    You can pretend you bought them like that

He texts me a photo of himself in new jeans:

    New jeans for America!
                    so american

    Didn't even try em on and they fit
    like jeans that fit really well

                  i'm sure if i think about it some
                  that will turn out to be a metaphor for murica

    Everything is a metaphor for
    everything else Sue!

Freezing jeans instead of washing them
               says something about your capacity for love
My mother's coworker's daughter
coming back from study abroad in the US

with $200 jeans for the whole family
            says something about imperialism
            and love. My favorite jeans, $15, shout
about my health, the thigh gap covered by those jeans
hovers over the morning Mississippi water.
                    The first pair of jeans I bought
                    at age eleven
had white horizontal streaks at the flared bottoms
because they were in fashion which says
            something about me and my friends
            flapping through school like baby sharks

in unspoken public school uniform, jeans and low-top sneakers
which we later replaced with jeans and brown suede mules
            which announced our seats on the orchestra

I've stopped feeling funny about how jeans
            are plural
I don't wear them often, which lets people know
I have learned to embrace my legs
                    sometimes literally, sitting outside
            staring blankly at the backyard, an activity we call
            gazing into the abyss which tells you
                        something about our coffee consumption

One summer evening we sat outside with beers
            watching the cat stalk something
Luke in a plaid shirt and baseball cap
                            and jeans, smoking a cigarette
and I in almost nothing, my bare feet resting
            on top of his sneakers
                        I felt the abyss embrace us
                        friendly and familiar

which says to me   I never stopped being the kind of person
who wears jeans
          if by jeans you mean uniform
            if uniform means clothing not for yourself

SLOWLY THE MILITARY INVADES EVERYONE

          March
They go. They go away for two years   and come back
grown up. The boy band members shave their heads
          and go. My baby uncle goes away,
comes back with an appendectomy scar,
hideous, quick military operation.   Someone says
conscription should be phased out. North Korea
coughs. No one suggests it again.

Most men report for mandatory military service
when still young enough   to bear it. On the news,
carted in buses to stop riots   in trucks to shoot deserters
round faces in sturdy glasses. Skip your salt ration
faint from exhaustion.   No one tries twice.
Put through their paces (shoot at). Endless messes
(filth & food).   On patrol   the North country
close enough to walk into.   Wouldn't they want you, young man?
Hands laced behind heads.   The dangerous ones grow shadows.

My father was excused. Engineers will not be lost
          to the battlefield. In high school   he learned
how to parade with plastic rifle.   Two weeks' bootcamp
when he was 30. Boots on the porch   large enough
to fit both my feet in one.

          My baby cousins go.
My second youngest's tattooed back
makes him ineligible for anything better   than basic infantry.
He'll suffer more   than the oldest, on break from aviation school
now stationed in Seoul. His parents drive past his guardhouse
just to see.

April
The Sinking of the Sewol

The newsreaders use an artificially correct accent
and a vocabulary I can't understand
Prayers on the beach
bowing towards the sea

I am instructed not to speak of it
with the children I teach
They tell me anyway
There was a school trip
on that ferry. Imagine
if all your school friends died
Imagine if that were us

May
There are 172 survivors
171 not counting the vice principal
who hanged himself for having been rescued
There are bodies who must be identified
by DNA   There are missing
who will be forever missing
President Park   (the daughter)   apologizes
for almost 300 deaths
most of the junior class of Danwon High School
The protesters wear yellow shirts   The soldiers surrounding them
wear yellow protective vests

June
One dangerous one   family name of Im
loose near the border   with ammunition
He has shot dead five other soldiers   He may defect
The soldiers sent to kill him could be
(but aren't)   my cousins

At the end of his service   my uncle
                    was asked to stay on as sniper
Remembering the 1980 massacre of civilians
        after the assassination of President Park
        (the father)   he declined

      July
We visit my father's alma mater
                  the best university in South Korea
                  the ugliest   inconvenient to reach
                  built away from the subway
                  so student protesters couldn't escape underground
            when the soldiers arrived   *Did you protest?*
No, I was too busy studying   (weapons engineering)

      August
My cousin comes home   on weekend leave
                  my last weekend here   the last family fathering
                where our grandmother will remember us
                Each time she looks at him she is surprised
                by how tanned he is   forgetting what he is
He dresses impeccably just in case a superior officer
sees him in public   and takes down his name

GEN √2

Gen 1.0 = *i*mmigrant

                                           Gen 1.5 = bicultural teen *i*mmigrant

Gen 2.0 = children of 1.0

∞

$\sqrt{2} = 2^{1/2} =$

1.41421356237309504880168872420969807856967187537694807317667973799…
= ambulatory limbo
       foreigner wherever I go
              2 cultures and remainder
                     gen irrational
                           too long to summarize
                                (summarise
                                I want to say)
= did I slide my passports across bulletproof plastic in exchange for new nationality & accent or are they still stored in silk

-   \\   in the infinite inexpressible number is hidden my birthdate written both ways
  [19901119 & 11191990]
  [the longitudes & latitudes of everywhere]

-   \\   if the number were written on a ribbon tied to the handle of my suitcase and unfurled
  [every bite of breath encoded would be there also]
  [incomprehensible but real]

THE BEAUTIFUL COUNTRY

mi: beauty. Not used by itself
but to form other Korean words such as
miin: beautiful person
misul: fine art
miguk: the United States of America.
No, really. Chinese does the same: měiguó

So: there are literally billions of people
who have this association, USA:
beautiful country, whether we like or believe
it or not —I believe it
sometimes but in those moods
I believe it of the universe

At first you don't know it
the same way American children don't know
the Latin roots of their words
I made the connection
when I was eight but it was meaningless
then America you were so distant
you might as well have been Narnia

Okay so usage transcends
etymology right like when we say
someone's sinister we're usually not
maligning left-handedness

but the beautiful country is so
plain and open
I mean its meaning

& every time someone complains in Korean
about the American military presence
or the hegemony of American media
the automatic translator in my brain
whispers: beautiful country

it's seriously annoying
but what else can we say? How else
to sum up this place
where I live & vote —I became
a citizen: simin, literally city person,
on October 10, 2013, that was
the year I graduated college from St. Louis,
a year before Ferguson, a month before Jonathan Ferrell,
the year of Obama's second inauguration, Boston
Marathon bombings, George Zimmerman's
acquittal, Detroit bankruptcy, debt-ceiling crisis,
I knew what I was getting into they made it
unnavigably difficult too they lost my paperwork
I complained it was like they were trying
to dissuade me from citizenship
I could have moved back to Korea
or emigrated someplace new
but I voluntarily committed myself to America

Sometimes I feel like I live
in a suburb painted on top
of a Roadrunner cartoon sometimes
the mountain behind my house is a golem
awake but lazing in bed
sometimes on the bus someone
says something ugly to me & I wonder if they

would say the same or nothing
if they knew I was / we were
citizens of the beautiful country
sometimes someone demands to know
what type of Asian I am
before they will speak to me
sometimes I am greeted
in the wrong Asian language
poorly pronounced which feels less rude
even though it involves more assumptions
sometimes the beautiful people
eat foreign words first cautious italics
attempts at making the right vowel sounds
soon abandoned & this used to bother me
not anymore say it I'm from Soul I'm a miguksimin

THE DRILL

There are fifteen minutes left when the PA system announces an armed intruder drill. Can we delay for five minutes while I double check my answers, says the valedictorian. Turn your papers face down, says the Statistics teacher, taping black construction paper over the glass panel in the door.

The students push their desks to the walls on either side of the door and crouch under the desks. The teacher turns off the lights and stands in the doorway to check whether they are in immediate shooting range. You fail, I can see everybody, she says. Now someone has to get shot. Who wants to volunteer?

The valedictorian and salutatorian look at each other. Everyone avoids eye contact with the teacher. Finally the valedictorian's best friend says, I can do it. I'm only ranked twelfth. Okay, you're going to die in the ambulance, says the teacher. She gives the twelfth a teddy bear and a bouquet of pink lilies. My favorite, says the twelfth.

The valedictorian starts screaming. It should have been you, she says to the salutatorian, everyone knows your top school's only Yale, you don't even want to be a doctor. To the twelfth she wails, I'll dedicate my speech to you, we'll talk about you at graduation so much you'll be practically top ten.

There are two clinical rotation students in the hallway with a stretcher. Hi Nurse Ryan, says the twelfth. This is a running joke, because everyone knows he's only a nursing assistant.

Her mother parks illegally in the bus lane. Should I cancel your SAT tutoring session, she shouts to the twelfth. It's too late for a refund, says the twelfth, sailing past on the stretcher. She can see a freshman sitting in the mouth of an ambulance, clipping on hair extensions then pulling them off to simulate traumatic hair loss and crying real tears: What if someone forgets to tell my teachers this is an excused absence?

HIGH SCHOOL BIOLOGY

I.

I wasn't fucking anybody, nor were any of my friends. I was learning to drive in a Jeep, which was the most Texan thing I ever did after saying y'all. I cried a lot because my father kept using the formal Korean for left and right, and my brain couldn't translate fast enough. Math and science were also hard, but I still got As in them because the thought of not getting all As gave me a feeling of doom like watching the sky turn green before a tornado. I didn't understand anything, I just memorized. Back then I would have used a semicolon in that sentence because the SATs test for comma splices. There was nothing my parents could do to punish me because I never went anywhere or received pocket money or watched television during the school year. I punished myself, walking in large Ls in my L-shaped room for hours. I taped a sign next to my bed saying WAIT ONE MORE YEAR to trick myself into postponing suicide. I woke with a swollen throat and thought: missing class=missing lesson=failing test=failing class=failing school=failing to get into a good college=failing life. I thought: this logic is as bad as Gregor Samsa's. I went to school anyway, as did my friends, which is why we shared the same illnesses.

II.

For the dissection project we had our pick of stiff cats in plastic sacks. I chose the largest cat, with thick black fur, wet with formalin. The first day I poked around for its salivary glands, reached into its eye socket to pull down the nictitating membrane. A week in, there were chunks of loose flesh like tinned tuna, crammed back into the open cavity at random. We moved down systematically, so the cat was sexless until the last day, when I dug out its fallopian tubes.

III.

I did things that were supposed to make me happy in a hypothetical future. I knew I wasn't happy, but sometimes I couldn't name what I was feeling, like when I was driving to the parking lot in the driving school convertible, top down, hair flying into sunset, after I failed the license test. Or coming home from school and gently palpitating my purring cat. *This is your liver. It has five lobes.* Or knowing how to draw a labeled diagram of a virus and still letting my grandmother stab the meat of my thumb with the needle she had used for thirty years to cure everyone's indigestion. Or singing the quadratic formula to the tune of Pop Goes the Weasel. Or accidentally leaving the corsage at my prom date's house, which he kept in the fridge, waiting for me to pick it up, which I never did. When I lifted my head from my anatomy test, people sitting in front of me were running their palms over their skulls and legs, as though reminding themselves of their own bodies would help them remember. I flattened my hair over my temporal lobes and double-checked my answers.

THERE BUT FOR THE GRACE

He said At least you're not married to William S Burroughs

I said That's a really low bar Jesus

*

For some years I lived with a man who gave me everything I wanted except regular contact with the outside world

*

I'm just saying lots of women have it worse he keeps you in his house he brings you cooked food what more do you want

*

The man was a restaurateur: sports bar, two locations, both successful. He said since he did the grocery shopping and drove me in his nice Lexus for dining out and shopping and fun stuff on his days off I wouldn't need a car of my own would I

*

At least you're not Joan of Arc

*

I spent my days in the basement watching television with a faceless hallucination I called Jesus so that if anybody overheard me talking to him it would have been as if I were praying

*

I took comfort in his small kindnesses

*

At least you're not a bride of Christ; the pleasures of the flesh are ripe

*

He spread his hand on my torso his fingers fitting between my ribs and said I want you to be happy with me

*

His house was in the heart of Texas the part of Texas where you drive half a day to get to anywhere that isn't Texas usually to Shreveport to play Texas Hold 'Em

*

At least you're not Mary Magdalene, you with your nape kissed through your hair every night

*

Jesus the number of hours I spend watching TV is inversely proportional to my happiness

*

He said If you were really unhappy you would walk out barefoot

But the asphalt would burn my soles and it would be weeks before I met anybody I knew

*

He took me to a hotel room and left me there while he went to gamble because I was too young to be admitted to the casino floor

*

He said At least you're not married to Bobby Brown

*

I'm no martyr I believe in nothing let me go

THE FLAMMABLE CITY

The most perfect city in the world
casts shadows on lesser cities
as it floats to the next convention

of beautiful things. It hums
and lathes in isolation, looking down
on the unplanned world. The most perfect

children surreptitiously throw
handmade confetti into the external
vents, not knowing they'll land

soggy clumps in oceans.
The most perfect parents encourage
the most perfect children to make-believe:

the below people walk without lifting
their soles from earth; the below
people eat earth

dissolved in seawater; the seas grow
engines of salt and walk ashore to eat
the below people.

The most perfect mayor in the world
takes daily walks in the symmetrical
marketplace. *Buckle up*, he says

to a young birdkeeper whose lungs
are flawed. *What is imperfect
shall be burned away.*

THE PRACTICAL TABLE OF ELEMENTS

The naked bottle marked BORON came out whenever we spotted a speck of ant in the house. I knew just enough chemistry to recognize the element name but not that what we used to kill was boric acid, that boron is a cosmic metal, glimmering gray like frozen mercury. They said elements make up everything, so pure elements must be everywhere, metal sweat of boron bottled, powdered sulfur underfoot, almost visible waves of oxygen rustling the lemongrass, a sheet of silicon in the bathroom as hand mirror—a leaving-present from Samsung to my father, who said you can find all the periodic table in semiconductors. I wrote in pencil, smearing carbon on my little finger, the English names of planets next to the Korean: Mercury, water planet; Venus, gold planet. Earth. Earth.

AMERICANA

being newly in love with an American i can't help
loving America too

i want to do all the American things
Americans do in movies

take a road trip

put my torso thru the sunroof to shout
into the highway
pointing west baby west

stop at a diner, a tired waitress serving
a slice of some sort of fruit pie
out of a glass case

i know this, i know you
like i know what a windmill sounds like
creaking across an American ranch

as vivid as any memory
i've never had

and when you hold the door and i step thru
people will stare but that's okay
because your big midwestern face
will follow me in

OURLAND

When you immigrate to our land, you must learn our language.
We do not say *my*. My parents do not exist,
nor my husband, my children, my house,
my family, my country. We are one people. Therefore,
you must tell me about our mother's health, and I'll reply
with our mother's new doctor. Together
we'll manage the mathematical business
of marrying our son and our daughter. Will our family buy them
a new house in our neighborhood? Yes. We'll tell our grandchildren
our folk tales. Oh, the tiger is coming down the mountain
to carry away our baby by the neck. Oh, our military keeps us safe
from communism. Oh, our brother has died shamefully,
so we erase him. When you've replaced your foreign clothes
with better ones, you won't notice how our tongues mimic
the shapes of our alphabet. As long as we give ourselves away,
we have nothing to fear.

WE THE PRESIDENT

after Choe Ha-rim

are a body divided, we know
what's right, and who's in charge,
we support education reform, we
build universities in remote places,
so we can't run, we send in,
the riot police, we march,
in jeans, we are bused away,
we come back fucked up,
we don't come back, we do not say,
anything, on television,
in newspapers, we install,
brilliant lights, in the censors'
offices, we gasp, crawling,
to City Hall, we get our manuscripts
back, saturated black, we,
ban private gatherings, of more,
than ten people, we meet,
a woman, striding through,
the courthouse, ceramic knife,
in tall boots, we are,
at truce, we are tensed,
we aim to improve, this,
is a self-coup, we, traitors,

ANNIVERSARY

October 10, 2016

I'm a three-year-old American today. Ten out of ten.
Your friends say you should take me to the state fair,
stop for gas station hot dogs on the way. Eat
some barbecue, taquitos, milkshakes.
They share a joint and distill America
into food and football.

I don't say: I prefer hockey; I actually like
cheap hot dogs; tonight, on our way home,
we'll get breakfast burritos for dinner.
I wonder what it's like

to be an old American, who's forgotten
or never knew a world that wasn't American,
saturated with guarantees.

I feel half-alive—death isn't personified
in my mind; is rather a place, from which I come,
and if I fall over, the ground will open like eggshell.

In a previous life, I was born with a blue Mongolian spot,
given to me by the Korean spirit
who shoves babies out of the womb.
The bruise faded in childhood. Nothing's permanent:

human rights, due process, fair elections,
stable currency, family, crisp folds in the flags, you.

Handholder, sleepsharer,
patron of the arts, night smoker,
caresser, when you pull up
at the drive-thru liquor store

what does the man passing you cigarettes and change
think of me, fingertips on your sleeve, feeling uselessly young?

Do we look good together? Do we look right?

I'm stamped all over with promises. Can you see them?
Will they rub away with time? When I'm so old
I stop keeping track of anniversaries,

will I still live in the same world, my ballot
in the mail, my tattoo sharp black, my hand
still pleasant to the touch?

RICOCHET

This, too, is truce
Country—for as long as I've lived
In Second Amendment land
Guns were boogeymen. Now, as I adjust

The stock of the pellet gun
Against my right shoulder, I think—
Maybe I should learn to shoot
For real. You make sure the cat
Is locked inside—I should aim higher.
I close my left eye—Birds
In the dying tree. The pellet
Goes into metal and out of metal
With two noises I perceive
As simultaneous—Will it go through hands?

The pellet lands in dirt—This weight feels good
For the same reasons guns frighten me. Nothing
Has changed, except now I live in a new reality
In which I exist between shots,

Always looking in the corner,
Asking where it's pointed, the safety,
What to shoot. There's always something to shoot.

And all this because of a nothing gun,
Even though, if one could be induced
To stand still, a raccoon or dog
Could die, horribly, at the end
Of my neon sight.

No matter how steadily I aim,
Taking my time, exercising more
Patience than I ever have
With cars and knives, I
Might miss—hit the fence, the shed—
This might turn on me—as anything can,
Such as my love for the owner
Of this pellet gun—What a strange person
I've become, a woman
In a red dress, shooting coke cans barefoot
In the backyard of a beloved,
Possessed by fear of power and freedom
To turn around and blind the beloved,

Who trusts I know what to do when the shots
Run out—The lead pellets calm in a patriotic tin,
Reloading 12 Destroyers, 12 doves dropping,
12 dents in dirt, 12 silent sentences
Of faith you put in me
And I in the section of the universe
In my sight, knowing
The risk we take.

NOTES

'Misremembrance'
Pietà, directed by Kim Ki-duk, was released by Drafthouse Films in 2013 in the United States.

'Tooth-Sized Joys'
The quotation "when the poison reaches the heart, that will be the end" is from Plato's *Phaedo* translated by Benjamin Jowett.

'Beautiful Country'
Seoul is deliberately misspelled to match the way English speakers pronounce Seoul as Soul.

'The Drill' is modeled after Russell Edson.

'Ourland'
Korean has the pronoun *my* but often uses *our* in places where English would use *my*, such as commonly referring to Korea as Our Country. The examples given here are all taken from Korean.